QUESTIONS

A family tree

QUESTIONS

A Mothers Journey from Anger and Grief to

Forgiveness

Peggy A. Hoard

Paws Printing

Marion, MI. 49665

QUESTIONS

This is a true story. Some of the names and locations have been changed to protect the privacy of individuals.

Books by Peggy A. Hoard

Christmas Skits 2014

This book may be ordered through Amazon, and directly from the author at: peggyhoard.com

ISBN-13: 978-0692248904
ISBN-10: 0692248900
Library of Congress Control Number: Pending
Printed in the United States of America

DEDICATION

This book is dedicated to my son, Patrick,

who has struggled with the loss of his

brother for years.

CONTENTS

FOREWORD

Every life is sacred to God and to that person whose life it is. The lives of individual people are sacred to parents, siblings, lovers, friends and most other people. Sometimes, however, we find people who are not able to keep that simple fact in mind in their relationships with others. When their lack of sensitivity to the feelings of others causes tragic consequences, the effects can rock not only their world but the world of those who do remember that lives are sacred. For some, those effects may dissipate with time, but for others, the pain can last a lifetime.

This story tells of a delightful and sensitive young man who brought joy and support to his parents and brother and who, in just 18 short years, had endeared himself to the community where he lived. It became his fate to become emotionally dependent upon young people so caught in the confusion of maturing that his life was not held sacred.

As his youthful dreams ended, his family's dreams became a nightmare of grief, anger, anxiety, guilt, and resentment. The paths they take to an acceptance of their family's fate take many routes. The more promising avenue led to the ability to forgive themselves and the other people involved in the loss of their loved one.

This is a true story with which we can all identify. We have all grieved when a loved one has been injured by the callousness of others. Haven't we all suffered from the painful emotions of resentment and anger, sometimes finding those feelings deepening into the bitterness of unforgiveness with its many destructive side effects?

Surrounded by the ambiance of God's love, experienced in the physical world through the support of her loved ones, friends, and church, Mrs. Hoard worked unflinchingly on understanding the feelings she was experiencing while supporting her family members in their grief. She finally experienced peace when she found herself embraced in a spiritual encounter with the Almighty.

Yvonne C. Hebert, MA

PREFACE

Dear Reader,

Thank you for considering my book for your reading enjoyment.

It has taken twenty-six years to write the story of my son's death. To go on living was, and at times, still is a daily struggle. I not only had to stay strong for myself, but also to help my family. We constantly had to cope with our painful feelings and accept his death.

In my opinion, suicide is the cruelest form of death. It leaves you with so many unanswered questions and a heavy burden of guilt.

For me, it created hate for the girl involved, and for the others who took part in breaking his heart.

My hope is that telling my son's tragedy will alert you to the effects of bullying, cruel jokes, and tender hearts. I hope you will find comfort in discovering how I forgave. I also hope that you will find solace and the support to continue living if someone you know commits suicide.

Peggy A. Hoard
07-01-2014

ACKNOWLEDGMENTS

I would like to thank my very good friend, Randy Johnston, for her continual encouragement. Not only did she encourage me to join her writers' group, but also to write the story of my son's death. She assisted with every step I took: writing it on paper, typing, critique, format, publishing and printing.

I also would like to thank my writers' group WTP (Write to Publish); especially Yvonne Hebert who believed my story should be told. I also thank my other writers' group Illuminovelists. The writers in both groups encouraged and critiqued my writings.

I also thank my wonderful friend, Merry Cook, who encouraged me to write, and supported my efforts.

I thank my husband, Bob, for his love and encouragement in everything I choose to do, especially my writing.

I thank God for giving me peace and forgiveness so I could go on with living.

Beloved, think it not strange
concerning the fiery trial which is to
try you, as though some strange thing
happened unto you:
But rejoice, inasmuch as ye are
partakers of Christ's sufferings; that,
when his glory shall be revealed, ye
may be glad also with exceeding joy.

I Peter 4: 12, 13

Chapter 1
The Incident

Meagan quickly dried her hands and answered the phone. "Hello," she answered cheerfully.

"Let me talk with Alex!" Meagan's father, Tom, demanded his voice strangely forceful.

"Dad, is something wrong?"

"I need to talk to Alex now!" His words were abrupt and full of what? Were they full of fear? She was a little hurt and wondered why he sounded so intense.

"Alex, telephone," she called to him.

He picked up the phone in the bedroom; a few seconds later he stood in the living room, with his jacket in one hand, and the other against his forehead. Giving him a puzzled look she placed her hands on her hips. She knew something was wrong, but she never expected what was coming.

"Your dad's on his way here," he said. "I'm meeting him out front." Alex sounded intense and factual. "He just received a strange phone call." Looking directly into her eyes, his voice became a whisper: "Someone is saying Drew's been shot."

Meagan's hand moved from her hip to her throat, she grabbed the doorway for support. The color drained from her face as questions filled her eyes.

"I can't tell you anything else. He doesn't know whether it's even true. We're going to try to find out what this is all about. Wait here and I'll call you as soon as I know something."

"Shot, what do you mean shot?" her eyes widened as her heart began to pound in her chest. "Alex? Alex! Where is he? How bad is he hurt?"

Her questions fell on deaf ears as he rushed into the garage, slamming the door shut behind him. Running to the living room window, she watched Alex leap into her dad's truck. In just seconds it had spun out of view. A thousand questions ran through her mind.

"Why couldn't I go too?" She thought anxiously. *"I'm his mom. I'm sure he will need me if he's been hurt."*

Jeff, her younger son, entered the room chuckling.

"What's going on mom? Wasn't that grandpa and Alex taking off? Man, you should have seen grandpa spinning gravel all over. What's going on mom?"

He froze when he saw the fear on her face.

"Oh Jeff, grandpa called and said Drew might have been shot!"

"Shot!" His eyes grew widened in surprise. "Who shot him mom? How did he get shot? Where is he? How bad is he hurt?"

She took her son's hand, pulling him to the davenport to sit. "All I know is grandpa called and said Drew might have been shot and he needed Alex to go with him. Jeff, please, I don't know any answers. I just know something has happened," she said, hot tears flowing down her cheeks. "I feel totally helpless being told to stay here. Stay here? Oh my gosh, Jeff, I can't just stay here waiting and do nothing. I've got to stay busy or I'll go crazy!"

"It will be OK mom." He wrapped his arms around her and squeezed, and he could feel her body tremble against him. "They'll take care of Drew; after all, Alex is a State Trooper! I'm sure they'll call soon and say it was just a bad joke someone's playing."

"I'm sure you're right." She mustered a smile and wiped the tears from her face. "I can't just sit. Let's find things to do to keep busy, too busy to think."

His face filled with concern. He was anxious to do anything that would help the situation. "OK mom, I'll stack the wood that's behind the house."

Meagan sat at the table recalling earlier in the day. It had been a beautiful fall day. She and Alex finished their weekend chores and were relaxing while gazing at the maple trees in their full glory of reds, oranges, and yellows.

"Maybe we should get married next fall instead of this January," Alex whispered.

Meagan smiled: "I don't want to wait a year to marry. Each of our past marriages was painful and our children, yours and mine, need to know what a good, loving marriage is like; a stable home filled with respect and love. No Alex, our lives are so good right now, I don't want to wait."

That was earlier, before the phone call, before her world stood still. Drying her tears she quickly stood and began to re-dust the dust-free furniture, and then stopped to look at the family photos on the wall. She touched Drew's band photo, remembering how proud he was when his group raised enough money to purchase new uniforms. He respected the band director and worked hard learning to read music and play the drums. Her stomach tightened into a knot as she fought tears.

When she could find nothing more to dust, she vacuumed the already clean floors and wiped down the spotless bathrooms. With nothing left to do in the house, she sat down at the kitchen table and rubbed her forehead. Frustration crept in.

"*Why,* " she wondered, "*why haven't they called or come back?*"

Her thoughts turned to Alex. They had met through mutual friends and had instantly fallen in love. They were able to talk about anything, everything without a worry about being ridiculed, belittled or abused. Life seemed solid and good, something to look forward to each day. She thought all was going so well.

"*Ring!*" She wanted to scream, glaring at the phone. Not knowing what else to do, she called the local hospital to inquire if Drew had been taken to the emergency room.

"I'm sorry; we don't have anyone here by that name."

Feeling relief and confusion at the same time, she paced the floor as questions continued to fill her mind.

"*Perhaps he was taken to a different hospital.*"

Rushing to the phone she dialed first one and then the other; but he wasn't at either of them. She felt encouraged, perhaps he wasn't hurt, and it was just a prank. But she had to know more.

She sat at the table for a few minutes but restlessly jumped up and paced the floor. Straightening the afghan on the back of the davenport, that wasn't crooked, then adjusting pictures on the wall, she would sit again. Raising her eyes to the telephone on the wall, she picked up the receiver and dialed the county sheriff's department. Meagan recognized the deputy's voice as a local girl. She felt hope of finding answers, any answers.

"Hello Beth, this is Meagan, Meagan Duncan. Can you tell me if you received a call regarding my son, Drew Davis tonight?"

"The only thing I can tell you right now Meagan, is that we have received a call that there was an incident."

"An incident? What kind of incident? Is he hurt? Do you know what happened?"

With each question her voice increased in urgency and demand. Her stomach tightened, and her breathing increased while pressing the receiver tighter to her ear.

"I can't tell you anything," Beth apologized. "I'm sorry Meagan, but please understand that I don't have any further information right now."

"Then please, please, call me if you hear anything more. I need to know if he's hurt and if he is, how bad he's hurt and where he is."

"I understand Meagan."

She stared at the receiver, listening to the dial tone. Panic started to build deeper inside. She took her purse to the car and opened the garage door. She wanted to be ready to go as soon as she received word where Drew was. She went back inside and continued to pace the floor. Once again she called the Sheriff's Office. The same deputy answered the phone.

"But please," she plead, "I know I'm expected to wait, but I have to know where Drew is and what's going on."

"I now know that the incident didn't happen in this county Meagan. It was in Blair County" Deputy Beth Rivers replied.

"You'll have to contact them. I have the phone number if you want it."

She slid onto the chair as her knees became too weak to hold her.

"Yes, please," she whispered. Her hand shook making it difficult to write. Taking a deep breath she dialed the numbers.

"Blair County Sheriff's Office, how can I help you?"

"Please, can you tell me how Drew Davis is, and what has happened?" Her words rushed together. "I'm his mother; and I'm trying to find out where he's been taken."

"I'm sorry," the deputy replied, "We're not handling this case, the State Police out of Carson are."

"I don't understand," Meagan questioned, "I was told that you were."

"A Trooper from their district was first on the scene; therefore, they're in charge. You'll have to call them. Can I give you the Post phone number?"

Meagan's voice began shaking so hard she could hardly be understood.

"I, I…I know the number…. but…. thank you."

"*Of course, there was a State Trooper on the scene. ALEX!*" Her mind raced, "*Why hadn't she thought of calling the Post earlier?*" Tears fell as she tried several times to dial the numbers correctly.

"Carson State Police, Trooper Jackson, can I help you?"

"Yes," she struggled to keep her voice under control. "This is Meagan Duncan. I'm calling for information about my son, Drew Davis. Something happened tonight, and I am trying to find out where he is. Alex Howard is on the scene, but hasn't been able to contact me yet," she sobbed.

"I'm sorry, Meagan." The trooper replied, with compassion. "Detective Cambs just left for the scene. I can't tell you anything until he returns. Wait for Alex, Meagan. I know he will contact you as soon as possible."

"Dear God, can't I get any answers?" Her chest burned with anger and fear. She called the Sheriff's Office, her voice a whisper.

"Beth, please, please tell me about my son. I keep being told to call here, and call there, and yet no one will tell me anything!"

Reluctantly Beth replied: "Meagan, I can't tell you much, but it doesn't look good."

As she hung up the phone the words rang over and over in her ears "it doesn't look good, it doesn't look good."

She sank onto the chair. It was now 9:00 pm-- three agonizing hours since the first call from her dad.

Hearing a vehicle pull into the driveway, she rushed outside. It was her father, and he was without Alex.

"Where was Alex"?

And if children, then heirs; heirs of
God and joint-heirs with Christ; if so
be that we suffer with him, that we
may be also be glorified together.
Romans 8:17

Chapter 2
The Answer

"Where have they taken Drew? I'm ready, I can leave right now and Jeff can go with you."

The truck engine went silent. At that moment, Meagan froze in motion. The only sounds were the tree frogs singing. Jeff came around the corner of the garage and slowly stopped, watching them, sensing the tension between them.

The truck door slowly opened and her dad stepped out. She looked into his eyes and backed up. As he stepped forward she retreated shaking her head no. When he reached his hand out to her, she turned and ran into the shelter of the house still shaking her head and saying over and over again - No! No! No!"

"Meg, I am so sorry. Drew is dead!" he sobbed, following her into the living room. "How can I tell his grandmother? This will just kill her. How can I go up the road and face her and tell her he is gone?"

"Dead? Dead?" The words echoed in Meagan's head. She cried: "Dear God no! NO! No!"

Falling to his knees, he put his hands over his face and started to sob. Meagan's mind froze. Her heart felt as if it were going to rip her chest apart. Her ears and eyes hurt. Her dad's sobbing interrupted her thoughts. She ached for him, her big, strong, tough dad sobbing in despair.

"It will be okay dad, it will be okay." Meagan wrapped her arms around him, and gently rocked.

Looking up, her heart broke again as she looked into Jeff's eyes. He had followed them into the house and now knew his brother was dead. Tears poured down both their faces.

She helped her dad to his feet and walked him to the truck. Her mom and Drew had developed a very special bond over the past eighteen years. Meagan wrapped her arms around herself, shivering at the thought of her dad facing her mom and breaking the news.

She couldn't stand the image of her mother's reaction, "*I just won't think about that right now.*"

"Mom, I want to go down the road to be with David." Jeff spoke carefully, but she could feel the pain in his voice. "You know he's one of Drew's best friends, and, well, I just want to be with one of his friends."

No, she didn't understand, but then, she didn't understand anything that had taken place. Suffering was visible in his eyes.

She wanted him to stay with her, within her sight, yet tried to understand his needs.

"Alright, but promise you will stay there and not go anywhere else."

Alone and afraid, she called her friend Ginny, and asked her to come sit with her until Alex could return. Meagan shivered, pacing the floor, unwilling to get far from the phone.

"Once again I'm left alone and expected to be the strong one, the tough one who can handle anything. I've always put what I couldn't handle today on the back burner. I would keep it there until I could deal with it. They are wrong this time. I'm not strong, I need them. I need all the help I can find."

"What happened? How did it happen? Where did it happen? Why did it happen?" Questions filled her head.

She then questioned herself if she really wanted to know details, after all, could anything bring him back?

Her mind raced over the past few months. Drew had just turned eighteen years old and desperately wanted independence. He had moved out, trying to live on his own.

Meagan's mom and dad had found him living on the street and begged him to come and live with them. He agreed and went home with them that day. Meagan wasn't happy with the situation, but there was nothing she could do about it. Given a choice of Drew living on the street or staying with her mom and dad, she agreed the latter was the better. Her mom and dad were thrilled to have him.

Her father was extremely close to Drew. They were, in fact, best friends. He helped Drew get a job and purchased an old van for him to drive to and from work and school. He was preparing him for entering the military right after graduation.

"What if I had fought harder for him to stay here and not move out? What if I had a better paying job so I could buy him a car and other things he wanted? What if I had asked him to come and help me today when I saw him this morning? I had teased him about a bruise on his neck, telling him it looked like a hickey. I shouldn't have said anything about it. What if, what if, what if?"

Questions didn't help; they just made her head hurt worse and left her with more confusion. How much longer could she stand not knowing what had happened to her son?

A car door slammed and Ginny rushed in, her eyes wide with fear.

"Meagan, have you heard anything? How is Drew?"

"He's dead!" she sobbed. "Please stay with me Ginny! I just can't believe he's gone! Nothing makes sense and I have so many questions."

Ginny put on a pot of coffee, and then sat at the table. She said little, keeping the conversation light. Silence filled the room as tears fell down Meagan's face.

Several times the phone rang with friends calling about Drew. Meagan couldn't understand how so many people knew what had happened to him before she did. Why didn't anyone call her with the facts? Why was she left in the dark?

At about 11:00 p.m. the door opened. At last Alex was home! He looked at Meagan with tears in his eyes.

"I am so sorry Meg," he whispered. "I was too late to help him."

She rushed to him, sobbing, and he folded his arms around her.

"I have to go back to the scene. Being first officer I don't have a choice Meg, please understand, I have to be there. I'll be back as soon as possible. I just had to come for a minute to hold you."

"But Alex, I don't understand. What….?"

"Meg, I can't discuss anything right now. The detective is there, but until he determines what took place, nothing is known. I'm sorry, you'll have to be patient and wait." His eyes pleaded for understanding, and then he was gone.

Meagan and Ginny sat in silence, sipping their coffee. Meagan jumped when the door bell rang. Two friends came in, rushed over to Meagan and embraced her.

"We are so sorry to hear about Drew!"

"How on earth did you know about Drew?" Meagan asked, looking shocked.

"The police scanner," she replied, "my brother heard it, called my other brother in Pontiac and he called us. We rushed right over. Oh Meagan, our hearts are breaking for you! Please, let us know if there is anything we can do to help. We can't even imagine what you're going through."

Silence filled the air; heads were down to avoid eye contact. They didn't pry for information but stood with tears of sorrow falling, their arms around her.

"Please call us if we can help in any way Meagan." They squeezed her again, and then the door softly closed behind them.

A few minutes later, Meagan's oldest brother, Roy, and her dad walked into the house.

"I'm so sorry Meagan," Roy said, "I can't imagine what you're going through!"

"How did you know? How could you know? I just found out!"

"Dad's neighbors heard it on the scanner and went over to their house right away," Roy said, pointing to her father. "They called all the family for mom. Everyone is at moms right now."

Silence filled the room. Ginny quietly slipped out of the door leaving Meagan with her family.

Tears fell, noses and eyes were wiped, and thoughts were left unspoken. A few minutes later her brother and dad left.

"The neighbor called everyone but me. No one called me," she thought silently.

Her mind raced with questions of how so many people in so many places knew what had happened, and she, Drew's mother, was left with little information for hours.

At 1:30 a.m. two vehicles pulled into the driveway. Her other brother, Bill, walked in, followed by her father, Alex and a stranger.

The stranger introduced himself as Detective Cambs.

"I am so sorry about your loss. May I have a seat?" he asked.

Meagan looked from one face to the other searching for a hint of what was about to take place. Everyone looked sad and serious. She felt her stomach tighten, her mouth was dry.

"Yes, yes of course."

"Meagan, we are sure Drew's death was a suicide."

That I have great heaviness and
continual sorrow in my heart.
Romans 9:2

Chapter 3
Suicide

"What?" Meagan said as she jumped up. "What are you talking about? How can you be sure? I don't understand any of this! I don't believe it could be suicide! Drew would never hurt anyone!"

"Meagan," Detective Cambs said, "I am so sorry. The evidence leads me to believe there was only one shot fired."

"How do you know Drew fired it? Maybe someone else fired the gun?"

"The gun was fired at point- blank range straight through the temple. If someone else held the gun, the bullet most likely would have entered at an angle. I don't want to cause you more pain, but I have to ask more questions."

"Dear God, what could have ever driven him to this?" She wailed, collapsing into a chair. "Why? Why? He would never hurt anyone. I can't believe this is happening!"

Alex moved beside her, placing his hand on her shoulder.

"He apparently did this because of his girlfriend." Cambs explained. "Can you tell me everything you can remember about today with Drew? Take your time Meagan."

She looked quickly at her dad. His face was pale except around his eyes where he had been wiping tears.

"Meagan." Cambs called her name louder: "Meagan!"

"What? What did you say?" She asked startled.

"Can you tell me what took place today?" Cambs continued patiently, "Today with Drew? "

"I talked with Drew this morning when I was at moms. I teased him about a bruise on his neck," her voice faltered as she shook her head as if she were shaking cobwebs away. "That's all I can tell you. You will have to ask dad the rest because Drew is living with my mom and dad right now. I would have stayed longer and talked longer if I had known it was the last time. Do you understand what I mean? If I had known, if only I had known…."

"What can you tell me about the events of today?" Cambs turned towards her father.

"Drew helped me all morning around the place….like he always does." Seconds passed as he struggled to regain his composure. "He went over to his girlfriend Sheila's house in the early afternoon, and then he came home for supper. Drew told his grandma he had some cassettes to return to his best friend, Gary. Gary had come back to help his uncle finish moving their things. Drew asked grandma if he could use her car. She loved him so much."

Taking his handkerchief out of his back pocket, he wiped his eyes, blew his nose and then carefully folded and returned it.

"It was a small thing to her…to let him use her car. She noticed his eyes were red, but thought it was from working outside in the wind. She told him yes and to be careful. She didn't know anything was wrong...you understand? She would have asked him questions if she had understood he was sad.

"Just a few minutes later he left and then Sheila's mother called to say……to say that Drew had been shot…… and told me he was just around the corner from her, off M-61, at his friend Gary's."

Meagan sat on the edge of the chair, staring at her father.

"I called Alex and asked him to go with me. I needed someone to go with me, and with Alex, being a state trooper; I figured he would know what to do.

"When we got to Gary's, grandma's car was pulled into the driveway with the motor running, lights on and driver's door wide open. There was loud music playing from inside the house and people standing out in front talking, laughing and drinking." Tom openly sobbed, blew his nose and continued.

"Someone was moving things out of the house into a truck. We saw someone run up and kick……kick something on the ground in front of the car."

Tom shook his head, several sobs escaped as he struggled to gain his composure.

"When Alex and I walked to the front of the car," Tom took his handkerchief out again to dry his eyes, this time keeping it clenched in his hand. "We discovered... Drew. It was Drew someone ran up and kicked! He was lying face down in the driveway, like he was headed back to the car. He wasn't moving. Alex turned him over to check for a pulse... and that's when I saw my .45 under him. My .45! Alex said he was gone. Gone, his life was gone and my world stopped."

Meagan gasped as she stared at her dad. The words played over again in her mind: "my .45 was under him."

"No one there seemed concerned." He wiped his face and blew his nose. "The music continued playing, a guy kept moving things into the truck." Tom flung his arms to demonstrate.

"No one seemed to care. Alex handled everything and kept everyone away. I just walked to the corner of the yard playing the day's events over and over in my head. Drew would never hurt anyone.

"Why did he have my gun?" Tom muffled a sob and wiped away tears again. "I don't know. I'd been teaching him how to use it, how to clean it and take it apart so he would know all about it when he went into the Army after graduation. I keep my guns locked up. Well, all my guns except my .45, I keep it in my bedroom in my dresser drawer. Drew must have taken it when he came back home."

Again Meagan continued to stare in disbelief. She had no idea her dad had been teaching Drew anything about his .45.

"Next the deputy arrived, and then you. I can't believe it was suicide, he would have no reason." Tom put his hands over his face to silence his sobs.

Meagan remained seated, gripping the table edge so hard her rings cut into her finger. She was in a fog, the words sounded far away. Her head pounded, her chest ached as she listened, and mentally rejecting what she was hearing. She looked from person to person hoping to find someone that would tell her it was a mistake.

"Nothing else that you can think of that could have brought this on?" asked Detective Cambs.

"No," Tom replied, "Nothing I can think of. Gary was his best friend: Sheila was Drew's girlfriend. Gary and Sheila had been going together, but when Gary moved away they broke up and then Sheila started going with Drew. He seemed to really be taken by the girl. That's all I know." Tom looked down as he slowly shook his head in disbelief.

"Apparently everything that took place tonight had to do with Sheila," Detective Cambs said. "She told Drew that she had broken up with Gary, but she hadn't. Gary believed that Drew was trying to break them up, but he wasn't."

"But she was going with Drew!" Meagan interrupted. "Right, Dad? They were together last night, right? That's where he got the hickey on his neck! Right, Dad? Isn't that right?"

Her dad nodded his head.

"Well Sheila denied ever being with Drew." Cambs continued. "Gary got mad and accused Drew of trying to break them up and told him they weren't friends any longer. Gary said Drew looked like a sad puppy dog as he looked from one to the other with tears streaming down his face. He said to Gary "Do you mean we aren't friends any longer?""

"This is so hard to understand." Meagan moaned.

"Gary and Sheila yelled names at him, and then Sheila's mother came into the room screaming at Drew to get out of her house. Suddenly all three were yelling terrible things at Drew until he left in tears.

"Later in the day Gary's uncle reported that he was busy moving the remainder of their things out of the house, using a makeshift ramp from the house to the truck. He paused when he heard a car pull into the driveway. He saw Drew get out and asked him what he wanted. Drew replied he wanted to talk to Gary and Sheila together. The uncle told him he didn't have time for this crap and told him to get his ass out of there."

Detective Cambs turned and looked at Meagan. Her full attention was on her father.

"Drew reportedly said that he wasn't going to leave until he talked with Sheila and Gary together," Cambs continued. "At this point, Gary's uncle jumped off the ramp and started towards him.

"Drew then pulled the .45 out and pointed it towards the ground. The uncle took another step towards him, reaching for the gun. Drew yelled that nobody was going to hurt him again, and then he allegedly placed the weapon to his head and pulled the trigger.

"Meagan I'm sorry." Detective Cambs reached across the table and squeezed her hand.

"I'm trying to give you information that is factual and that will answer some of your questions. I know this is hard for you and I want to make it easier. I still have the investigation to complete so I can't tell you anything else until it's finished. I'll give you a copy of the full report when it is wrapped up. Right now, Meagan, I need your permission to make a phone call to the hospital and authorize them to release the body to the funeral home."

Meagan felt as if someone had just kicked her in the stomach. She looked at her dad. His shoulders were bent forward; he looked like a beaten man.

"How did he get your .45, dad?" She wanted to ask but couldn't bring herself to cause him more pain. So many questions swirled in her head: *"Where did he get the bullets? If you kept both locked in separate locations, how did he get the keys? Suicide, suicide? Drew is one of the gentlest people I know. He's the peacemaker, the one who opened the door for company and welcomed them in with a cup of coffee. He always took their coats and hung them in the closet. When I came home with groceries he was right there to help unload them."*

"Meagan," Detective called, "Meagan. Did you hear my question?"

"I'm sorry, what? No. No I guess I didn't hear you. What did you ask?"

"I said I could call the hospital. You could give your permission to release Drew's body over the phone."

"His body? His body?" she questioned, suddenly enveloped in horror at the thought of Drew's body being taken to a funeral home. It was all so final.

She looked at Alex, her eyes begging for direction. He nodded his head in agreement.

"Yes," she whispered, "yes, you can make the call."

Standing, she moved out of the way of the phone. Her knees were weak; her ears were filled with the sounds of the ocean, while she fought to keep nausea down.

"How can I give Drew to someone? What will they do with him? I just want to bring him home to me!"

The detective placed the call and then handed the receiver to Meagan. She looked first at the phone, then her dad, and then Alex. Alex nodded his head again for her to follow through.

"Hello," she whispered. "Yes, this is Meagan Duncan. Yes, you can give Drew to the funeral director."

"Thank you Meagan," Detective Cambs said, "I will contact you if I have any further questions. I am so sorry for your loss. Please call me if I can help."

He handed her his card and left. Her brother and her dad left a few minutes later.

Moments later her son, Jeff, rushed into the house, panting for breath.

"Mom who was just here?" What did you find out?"

"We don't have all the details Jeff, and we won't until the detective finished his report. We know everything involved Sheila"

"I knew it!" Jeff exploded, "I never trusted her. She was always flirting with all the guys whenever Gary wasn't around. I hate her!"

"Hold on, "Alex stated, "We don't have all the facts. We can't make unfair judgments until all the facts are in. Don't be upset with anyone Jeff, we all need to pull together to get through this."

"I don't know Alex," Jeff moaned, "I can't believe Drew would take his own life." Several sobs escaped: "I'm going to bed Mom, I'm whipped. See you in the morning."

Alex sat down across the table from her and gently clasped her hands. She looked into his eyes with questions.

"Tomorrow," Alex said, "We will talk about it tomorrow. Right now let's try to get some sleep."

Alex led Meagan to the bedroom. Sleep seemed impossible, yet when it came, it was a deep sleep.

Behold, we count them happy which endure.
Ye have heard of the patience of Job, and
have seen the end of the Lord: that the Lord
is very pitiful, and of tender mercy.
James 10:11

Chapter 4
Tomorrow

"Oh Alex, I just had the most horrible nightmare!" She leaned against his chest.

"Meagan, it wasn't a nightmare." Alex held her. "Drew is gone." His eyes were filled with pain.

"I don't understand," she moaned, "How could this happen?"

"Meagan, we don't know exactly what happened. We do know that it was over his girlfriend, Sheila, and his best friend, Gary. She apparently told Drew that she and Gary were split up, then she and Drew got involved."

"But she did go with Drew! I just teased him about the hickey on his neck, remember Alex?"

"Yes, I remember Meg. But when Gary came back to retrieve the rest of his things, he was unaware of Sheila and Drew's relationship. Drew got caught in the middle of her lie."

"Of course, she wanted Gary while he was here." Meg gasped. "But when he moved away she went after Drew. I think she never really broke up with Gary!"

"Well Meg, she did deny ever being with Drew. Apparently when Drew tried to explain the relationship he and Sheila had, she acted furious and called him a liar. She convinced Gary he was just trying to break them up. Gary believed her. Then everyone at the house joined and yelled unthinkable things at him, throwing him out."

"Oh poor Drew, my poor Drew. Why didn't he come to one of us? Why didn't he let us help him through this? Why didn't her mother have sympathy for him?"

"I don't know Meg. The family doesn't strike me as sensitive. Their language was pretty strong, and I didn't observe any sympathy towards Drew."

"I wish he had never gotten involved with Sheila or her family! In fact, I wish he'd never been friends with Gary! Are you sure he shot himself? Maybe the uncle shot him?"

"No, Meg, we know he went over there with your dad's .45. We're sure Drew fired the shot. We don't know if he was bumped or grabbed, if so, that could have made the gun go off. We'll probably never know everything that took place. But Meagan, we can be thankful he didn't shoot any of them. He had a full clip plus one in the chamber. He could have chosen to shoot everyone who was there."

"Oh dear God, I couldn't have lived through that. I couldn't handle Drew hurting others!"

"I know Meg, I know. Detective Cambs explained all he could last night. We just don't have all the answers yet. But I know we have to get through this. We have to go on.

"Come on, I'll make us coffee." He said as he gave her a tight squeeze.

Later in the morning, as she was doing laundry, her dad phoned. His voice was sober and strained.

"Meagan, we have to go to the funeral home and make arrangements for Drew. We need to be there at 11:00 a.m. this morning."

"OK dad," She softly replied, "I'll be ready."

"Mom, David's mother said I could spend whatever time I wanted to at their house." Jeff said as he came into the kitchen for breakfast. "Do you care if I spend the day there? I can just hang out, swim in the pool, and play video games with David."

Megan fought the instinct to grab his shoulders and shake him.

"*Do you understand I've lost one son and desperately need the other? Don't you understand I need you close by my side right now?*"

But she didn't say that, nor did she shake him. She looked into his eyes and could see the pain. Mustering a smile, she caressed his cheek with hand.

"Yes Jeff, you can spend the day with David. Remember to help around their house and be polite."

After breakfast Jeff packed a day bag, kissed Meg on the cheek and left for David's. She kept busy doing things around the house to keep her mind occupied. Everything seemed mechanical: making the bed, cleaning the kitchen and bathrooms.

Every time she passed Drew's room she would enter and look around. Going into the closet, she took out his Cub Scout uniform. Sitting on his bed, her fingers touched each patch recalling how Drew had earned it. She had been den mother for five years, what marvelous times their den experienced.

"Oh Drew, I remember how proud you were every time you earned an award. I remember how hard you worked to achieve each one," she wept with pride and loss.

Each week the boys in her troop got off the bus at her house. She greeted them with snacks and supplies in a bag. They hiked behind the house, around the pond, across the swinging bridge and into the woods. They worked so hard for their awards. Identifying leaves, rocks, and mosses were some of their many accomplishments.

The hardest project for Drew was macramé. His fingers just wouldn't cooperate with the knots, yet once he succeeded, he beamed with pride. She stood quickly when she noticed her tears had fallen on the blue shirt. She gave it one last caress as she replaced it back into the closet.

"Oh Drew, why?" she cried, as she looked at the painting on the wall. She recalled painting it for him when they were moving into this new home over ten years ago. It was mustard colored suede with a tiger lying under huge green ferns. She had split a bamboo fishing pole to make the frame. He had loved the painting, looking at it every night as he fell asleep. Tears fell quickly down her cheeks as her chest tightened with pain.

Wherefore let them that suffer according to the will of God commit the keeping of their souls to him in well doing, as unto the faithful Creator.
1 Peter 4:19

Chapter 5
Funeral Arrangements

It seemed just minutes had passed when Alex appeared suddenly in the doorway.

"It's time to leave for the funeral home," he said softly.

When they arrived, her mom and dad were already there, sitting in their car. Her mom could hardly speak, her voice was so strained.

The funeral director greeted them. With a soothing voice, he offered his sympathy for the loss of her son, and then became all business. They quietly followed him into another room to pick out the casket. Her dad wanted the best casket for Drew; he thought it was the last thing he could buy for him. Meagan didn't care what materials or color it was; she didn't want Drew in any of them.

Going back to the office, they chose a vault. Almost mechanically the director asked questions: which minister should perform the funeral; what days should they hold for visitation and the funeral; what music did they want played; whom did they want for pall bearers; what style of memory cards and thank you cards; who was to play the organ or piano at the funeral service; what did they want in the obituary for the newspapers; where would the luncheon be after the funeral; and how much money did they want in each envelope for each service performed and for the luncheon? The questions were endless, not allowing her time to think before answering.

The director instructed the family to bring in clothes and a set of new underwear for Drew. They were assured by him that Drew would look as if he were asleep. He said they would want to have a flower arrangement for the casket, and then he listed cost of each item. On and on, he brought up detail after detail. Meagan gripped Alex's arm as her head swirled with all the questions. Thankfully her dad quietly made most of the decisions, but always looked to her for approval.

"Will it ever end?" She thought repeatedly.

Finally, the arrangements complete, they walked out to their vehicles. Words were not exchanged. They just drove home.

As they entered the house, Meagan reminded Alex it was his oldest daughter's sixteenth birthday. The divorce had been especially hard on the children. He was still waiting for the judge's decision on custody of his two girls and who would obtain possession of their home and land.

"Alex, please go celebrate Shelly's birthday with her. This is such an important time for a young person. I'll be fine."

"Are you sure Meg? Shelly will understand if I stay here."

"No, I don't want her to know. She needs to be happy today, not sad. Just go and make her feel special and loved."

Meagan sat in the living room looking through family albums. She studied each photo, trying to find a flaw, a hint of sadness, a reason why Drew would end his life. She closed the albums after a few hours. Her head pounded, her chest ached. She still was without answers, just more questions.

Late in the afternoon Jeff returned home. Meagan was surprised when she realized it was meal time and quickly fixed supper, just as Alex returned from his daughter's birthday party. They all sat in silence, looking at their plates pushing their food around as if creating a design. After dinner, Jeff went to his room for the evening, Alex watched television, and Meg cleaned the kitchen, and then went to bed. She felt exhausted, drained of all her strength, yet sleep didn't come until Alex joined her.

Alex went on duty the next morning and Jeff needed to be with his friends. Meagan understood and allowed him to go. Once again she was alone; alone to cry, alone to think and ask all the questions with no answers. Her dad called and asked her to go with him to town and deliver the items requested by the funeral director, and to purchase a flower spray for the casket.

She gathered the clothes for Drew, carefully folding them and placing them in a bag. Her fingers caressed the shirt and pants. Drew didn't have anything fancy to wear: he had always been just a country boy with a deep love for nature and people. He loved the simple things in life: hunting, fishing, camping. He didn't need fancy now; he needed to just be himself.

"Be himself," she thought: *"I will take him any way I can get him. I just want him back!"*

When her dad arrived she hurried out to the truck. At the clothing store, they picked out a set of underwear then delivered everything to the funeral home. At the florist, they picked out the flowers for the casket with ribbons that read "Son," "Brother," "Grandson."

When her dad dropped Meagan off at home, hardly a dozen words had passed between them. He looked at her and his tears would start. She looked at him and her tears would start. There were no answers, only questions.

She had not been home long when the door bell rang. Opening the door, Meg came face to face with a co-worker, Carol. Tears pooled, and then flowed down her cheeks as she looked into Meagan's eyes.

"I'm so sorry Meagan. I don't know what to say or do. I feel helpless." She

54

placed a casserole dish into Meg's hands, covered her heart with her hand, and then fled.

Meagan placed the dish into the refrigerator, and then sat at the table. She wondered what she would say if the situation was reversed. Nothing can be done or said to undo what's been done.

An hour later the door bell rang. It was her neighbor.

"I'm so sorry Meagan. Drew was such a nice kid. I'm just so sorry. Please, call me if I can help in any way. I've made you a deli tray. It isn't much, but I hope it will help."

"Thank you Terri," Meagan hugged her. Tears fell as muffled sobs escaped; bodies trembled with heartbreaking emotion.

She put the deli ring in the fridge, and again sat down at the dining room table. Holding her head in her hands, she gazed out the window. There were so many memories of the activities in the back yard with the boys. A large sand pile, placed under the oak tree, was where the boys had played endless hours with Tonka toys. They built roads, towns, and tunnels with their machinery. Meagan heard their squeals of delight as they stomped everything into nonexistence, only to rebuild again the next day.

The swing set and slide provided hours of fun. She smiled reminiscing about the boys wanting to play outside after a rainstorm.

Finally, she had told them they could if they didn't get their clothes or shoes wet. It wasn't long before a neighbor telephoned informing her that the boys were buck naked in the back yard. She thanked him for his concern and went to the kitchen window. There they were, naked indeed, laughing and zipping down the slide as they landed in a huge puddle of water. On the picnic table sat their shoes and pile of neatly folded clothes. Meagan laughed at their cleverness and decided a bath would take care of the problem.

They are of the world: therefore speak they
of the world, and the world heareth them.
1 John 4:5

Chapter 6
Sheila's Mother

The doorbell rang suddenly, loudly. Meagan was shocked to see that it was Sheila's mother, Beth.

"Meagan," she pleaded, "my daughter is so broken up over this thing with Drew. I need you to call her and let her know nothing is her fault! She's blaming herself and is really upset!"

Meagan's mouth opened in surprise. She was stunned. Thoughts swirled in her head.

"My son is dead over something that happened at your home with your daughter and my son's best friend and you want ME to calm her and reassure HER that nothing is HER fault?"

Meagan's hand clutched the doorway to steady her swaying body.

"Beth, I can't help you now!" Her voice shook as she clutched the doorway tighter.

"You don't understand! I'm talking about my daughter," Beth yelled. "Your son is dead but my daughter is alive and needs help!"

"Please, please leave!" Meagan's body shook with rage.

Beth slammed the house door behind her and raced to her car. She spun out of the driveway, her tires throwing gravel everywhere.

"What else can happen to test my strength?" Meagan leaned against the wall. It felt cool to her aching head.

She remembered the detective describing the horrible things Gary, Sheila and her mother had yelled at Drew, throwing him out of their house.

"They kicked him as he lay dead on the cold ground and now they want my help? Sheila was Drew's first true love. She lied and denied any involvement with him."

Terrible pain formed in Meagan's stomach, a pain that felt like hate.

Over the next few days' phone calls poured in from family and friends expressing sympathy and shock over Drew's death. People brought casseroles to both Meagan and her parents. The local paper placed the news on the front page. The local TV stations aired it on the six o'clock news. No sympathy was addressed, no responsibility for the people involved in his death, no article on how lives would be changed…. forever…. just the facts….cold abbreviated facts.

The night before the funeral Meagan couldn't fall asleep. She tossed and turned until her body ached. Finally, she crept out of bed, closing the door behind her, and went quietly into the living room. So many thoughts crowded in her mind. The sorrow and agony on the faces of her parents and Jeff haunted her. Taking a tablet of paper and pen, she sat at the dining room table.

"I need to write something that will help them get through this, something from Drew that can be read at the funeral."

TO EVERYONE I LOVE
By Meagan Davis for Drew Davis

Please, don't torment yourself with the question "Why?"

You will never understand the reason I felt I needed to die.

Never blame yourself or anyone else for what I have done.

There is no one else who is at fault but me, no not even one.

Some people are stronger than others and are able to cope,

For me, I couldn't see tomorrow, I couldn't find any hope.

I wanted to do what was right and be with you every day,

I wanted to be there for you, but I just couldn't find the way.

Please, know that I never wanted to cause you pain or sorrow,

I just couldn't bring myself to face another tomorrow.

We can't change anything that has already taken place,

So for me, lift that chin up and put a smile upon your face.

Remember the good times we've shared and all the fun,

Look at the photos and laugh at the silly things that were done,

Go on with your living and do the very best that you can.

And if you fall down, jump up, brush yourself off, and try again.

Don't ever let this world get you down the way it did me,

For in you, everything good and wonderful is exactly what I see.

I am with you always, in your memories, and in your heart.

The bond that has grown between us can never come apart.

Don't dwell upon my death or stay sad for very long

Instead, Smile! Live! Laugh! And Hum a happy song

Don't ever doubt my love or how special you were to me,

You were everything I could have ever wanted a family to be.

The best way to always love me, is to continue living each day,

Walk with the Lord, help others and continue to pray.

Meg laid the tablet and pen on the table. Feeling drained of strength she returned to bed, and fell into a deep sleep.

Mercy unto you, and peace, and love, be
multiplied.
Jude 1:2

Chapter 7
Visitation

The next day Meagan and her family met at the funeral home to view Drew at 12:30 p.m. Meagan's knees were weak, her head hurt, her hands shook and her stomach ached as Alex led her up the steps to the funeral home. The director greeted them. The foyer smelled of flowers. Soft music played in the background. They turned and walked into the room that held the casket. She saw the opened guest book, envelopes arranged for donations, and many flowers and plants lining the room.

Meagan's hand gripped the doorway.

"I don't want to be here," she whispered.

Alex took her other hand, squeezing it as her parents went forward toward the casket. The sound of sobs filled the room. Once again she fought weak knees and sickness. Slowly Alex, Meagan and Jeff approached the casket.

Drew looked as if he were asleep. His usual bright smile was gone. His beautiful blue eyes were hidden behind closed eyelids. His blonde hair shone in the light. He looked sad. He didn't look as if he had been wounded. She thought of brushing his hair aside to see if indeed there was a bullet wound as she had been told, but thought better for fear of what she would find. She stared at her son, tears falling until Alex took her arm and led her aside. So many muffled sobs filled the room. She could identify each one, even with her eyes closed.

In just a few minutes, others would come and see Drew and pay their respects. They would see him so still, so quiet. Many did come-teachers from the elementary and high school, the career tech school, co-workers, family, friends, neighbors and his classmates, all with tears in their eyes; all with words of condolences and memories. Each person felt their own grief over such a senseless loss.

The line of mourners seemed to never end: seven o'clock came and went and it was close to nine before the last person left. Meagan didn't want to leave Drew, but everyone was exhausted and ready to go home. Tomorrow would be the funeral. Tomorrow would be the last time she would see her son.

The Lord is my shepherd; I shall not want.
He maketh me to lie down in green pastures:
he leadeth me beside the still waters.
He restoreth my soul: he leadeth me in the
paths of righteousness for his name's sake.
Yea, though I walk through the valley of the
shadow of death, I will fear no evil: for thou
art with me, they rod and they staff they
comfort me.
Thou preparest a table before me in the
presence of mine enemies: thou anointest
my head with oil; my cup runneth over.
Surely goodness and mercy shall follow me
all the days of my life: and I will dwell in
the house of the Lord for ever.
Psalm 23: 1-6

Chapter 8
The Funeral

At home, she and Alex sat on the couch staring, saying nothing. The telephone rang and thankfully Jeff answered it.

"Mom, dad wants to pick me up tomorrow morning, take me out for breakfast, and then to the funeral." he said, standing uncomfortably in front of her.

"Oh Jeff," she moaned, "don't you want to go with us?"

"I do Mom, but dad was crying. He wants me to be with him. He said he doesn't have anybody else. He said he really needs me, and you have Alex."

Her head pounded, she looked at the tears in his eyes and his hands fidgeting with the buttons on his shirt.

"If that is what you want to do Jeff."

"I'll call him right now!" Relief filled his face, his hands dropped to his side. "Thanks mom, this means so much to him."

She needed to be calm for Jeff; this was very traumatic and heartbreaking for him also. She didn't want to say or do anything to make his situation worse. He needed to return to school in a few days and face

Sheila and all the other kids. It wouldn't be easy for him.

Meagan bit her lower lip as she thought back to the years of verbal abuse both she and Drew had suffered from Jeff's dad. Drew was so thankful when the divorce was final.

"I don't know if I can get through tomorrow Alex," she said as she leaned her head on Alex's shoulder.

"We will get through this," he said as he placed his arm around her shoulder, "because we have to."

Jeff's dad arrived early the next morning, beeping his horn when pulling into the driveway. Jeff paused to give Meagan a kiss on the cheek, then rushed out to meet his father.

Meagan fumbled with the buttons on her dress. She couldn't stop her hands from shaking. Tears of frustration fell; she took several deep breaths trying to become calm.

"It's time to go Meg," Alex softly said as he entered the bedroom. His eyes filled with concern.

Friends drove them to the church. Her parents were there. The parking lot was full. Meagan's legs felt full of lead making each step difficult. Inside many people were seated, others were standing near Drew. A guest book was open on a lectern near the door. Flowers and arrangements crowded the altar. The spray of flowers she had chosen cascaded over the closed end of the casket.

Alex led Meagan to the front pew beside her parents. Her dad's shirt was wet from tears. Her mom sat like a stone, stiff, pale and sad. Soon the pews and extra chairs were filled. Additional chairs were set up in the fellowship hall. When they were filled, people stood along the walls.

Music played softly in the background as the Pastor walked to the altar. He read the poem she had written to give comfort to her mom, dad and Jeff. The words washed over her as the tides of the ocean.

"Oh Drew," she thought, *"What could I have I done differently? What should I have done? If only I could go back to... to when? What would have made a difference in your life? I would gladly have given my life for yours. I don't know if I can bear this Drew, I just don't know".*

Soon, too soon, people were leaving the church. She and Alex were the last to stand and approach the casket. She reached out, placing her hand on Drew's chest. How hard it was, no softness, no life in his body! She looked up at the funeral director and shook her head no. Tears streamed down her face as Alex tried to lead her away.

"NO!" Meagan cried, "NO!"

The director motioned for Alex to take her out. With one arm around her waist, Alex guided her to the car.

They got into the car just as the pall bearers were placing the casket into the hearse. Meagan clutched the back of the seat in front of her, straining to catch a glimpse of Drew, and then crumpled into the seat. As they drove from the church to the cemetery, Meagan turned to look out the window.

"How can people be walking down the street talking and laughing while Drew's life is over?" She wondered bitterly. *"How can the world go on? Don't they know life will never be the same? Don't they know what has happened?"*

She noticed a young girl and a boy about Drew's age, very interested in each other, holding hands, oblivious to anything around them, just themselves.

"That could be Drew with a girlfriend. I will never have a grandchild of Drew's. How cruel this life is. How could Sheila, Gary and Beth yell at him and call him names? How could Sheila deny being with him? Do some people lack compassion or love? Didn't they know how precious his life was?"

Once again she felt the barbs of hate pricking her heart.

At the cemetery, Meagan watched as they unloaded the casket and placed it on the grave site. The words the minister spoke sounded far off. Panic engulfed her as she thought about Drew being lowered into that dark hole never to be seen again. She thought of standing up and shouting for them to stop. She squeezed Alex's hand so tight it hurt her fingers.

"Dear God," she prayed, *"how am I going to make it? How can I let them put Drew down that dark hole? God, give me the power to do this!"*

Meagan leaned on Alex. People were crowding around her to offer their sympathy. So many people with tears in their eyes, with pain in their faces, yet each one gave her strength. She had placed most of what had happened on the back burner, but the burner was now full and overflowing.

"Why? Why?" The question kept pounding in her head as he turned to look at the casket one last time.

"How could you pull the trigger? How could you take yourself away from us? How could you leave us with such intense pain and so many questions? You were the kindest, most loving person I knew. I know you never would have wanted to intentionally hurt all of us this way. Why Drew, why?"

Ladies from the township served a funeral luncheon at the township hall.

"I don't want to go Alex, I'm not hungry."

"Meg, everyone is there, your parents, brothers and their families, friends, and Jeff. We need to go in. You need to be there, you don't have to eat, but you need to go in."

73

"Oh Alex, I'm exhausted! I don't want to face more people. I just want to be left alone!"

"And that's exactly why you need to go in Meg. Being alone is not going to help you heal. You need to be there for your parents and Jeff; you need to be there for you."

"All right," Meagan sighed, "but I don't want to stay any longer than I have to."

He led her inside where the people were sitting and visiting. At the far end sat her family. Meg sat at the end of the table, facing the door. She didn't go to the food table. Instead she sat with her head down, wiping tears that refused to cease.

Suddenly the laughter and talking stopped. Only the sound of dishes being scraped could be heard. Meagan looked up to see Jeff and his father standing in the doorway. Jeff looked at her with pleading eyes to do something to help the situation. He wrung his hands and shuffled his feet. His dad looked a fish out of water.

"Darn it!" Meagan thought. *Why did he have to come in here? He could have just dropped Jeff off and left. Doesn't he know Drew despised him as I do?"*

Looking again at Jeff, her heart softened. Standing, she walked to the end of the hall. Each step took effort. Her smile was forced, her shoulders back, her chin up, concealing her angry thoughts about his father. When she reached them, Jeff's father embraced her, sobbing on her shoulder, but she gently pushed from his embrace.

"Come in, have something to eat, and visit with the people you know," she requested calmly.

"Come on dad!" Jeff said, looking relieved.

Meagan quickly returned to her table. People approached sharing their memories, offering their sympathy and love. She felt free to leave when the last guest departed.

Have mercy upon me, O Lord, for I am in
trouble: mine eye is consumed with grief.
Psalm 31:9

Chapter 9
The Letters

At home, Jeff stood in the driveway.

"Are you OK, Jeff?"

"Yes Mom. Dad was in a hurry to get home, so he dropped me off and left. Thanks for making him feel welcome at the hall. I wanted him to come in and eat. He couldn't stop crying at the funeral and I felt so sorry for him."

"It's over now Jeff." Meagan's heart ached for her son. She felt rage at his dad and how he could still manipulate with his tears and sad stories. She recalled when Jeff was scheduled to live with his dad for the summer- it only lasted a month. One day his father drove in, threw all of Jeff's possessions on the lawn, told Jeff to get out and left. She felt relief that they were no longer under his abuse.

At home she excused herself and crawled into bed, drained of strength. She was trapped in a nightmare and didn't know how to escape. Her chest ached as if it had been physically beaten. Questions flooded her thoughts until she felt her head would explode.

The next day Jeff attended school, and Alex returned to work. Meagan went to her parents' home and wrote thank you notes. Once they were completed she entered the bedroom that had been Drew's. It looked as if he had just climbed out of bed. For several minutes she stood and let her eyes drink in every detail. Going to the bed, she sat, then leaned over, placing her face upon the pillow, and breathed in his scent. Clutching it tightly, she sat up and scanned the room.

The headboard contained three compartments. In one, she noticed a tablet of paper and pen. Picking it up, she began to read:

Dear Sheila,

Last night was wonderful! I love you so much! I can't wait until we can be together again. I'm sorry you're having trouble with your mom, but I'm sure it will get better. I think you are so beautiful. All I can think about is being with you.

The letter was unfinished. Meagan reread it several times before placing it back. Fresh tears fell as her heart ached.

"What a beautiful letter. He really loved her."

Taking a box she folded each item of clothing and carefully placing it inside. She noticed a folded piece of paper on the dresser and opened it:

Drew, I can't stand living in this d___ house another minute! I hate my f____mother and wish she was dead. I hate living here! I'll be glad when I can get the f____out! I love you so much and glad that d___ Gary is out of my life! I only stayed with him because he f___ing threatened me not to leave him. I feel safe with you Drew. Sheila

Meagan's hand shook as she folded the note and put it back. Her stomach tightened; anger seeped into her heart.

"How hateful Sheila's note was, and full of filthy language. So she did go with Drew and led him to believe she didn't want to be with Gary. No wonder he was confused when he found them together. Oh Drew, if only you had come to me and let me help you through the pain."

The second compartment held a small plain box. She gasped. Inside was what looked like two used condoms. Her mind raced until she recalled the hickey on Drew's neck.

"I *asked the boys not to have sex until they graduated from school, and when they did, to be sure they used protection to prevent the girl from getting pregnant. I had been specific on the consequences for all three: the boy, the girl and the unborn child. So Sheila was Drew's first love in more ways than one. At least he did use protection. I wonder if she even realizes the love and concern he had for her".*

Meagan carried the box of clothes into the dining room. Her dad wanted to give them to a boy Drew had been working with. He didn't have much and could use the boots and clothing. Nothing of Drew's could fit Jeff so Meagan agreed the things should go to someone who needed them.

Returning to Drew's room, she placed the few things from the third compartment in a small box to take home. A brass incense burner, sun glasses, scrap book and photo album. In a sack, she placed his school books to be returned to the high school. She looked for his wallet but couldn't find it. After making the bed, she carried the items out of the room and closed the door behind her.

"Mom, did dad get Drew's wallet?"

"No, he didn't get anything Meagan. He has torn the inside of Drew's van apart looking for a suicide note. He's looked everywhere! I told him that I didn't think Drew left one, because I don't think he planned on this. He won't listen to me. It's like he can't stop until he knows."

"I'll talk with him mom. Where is he right now?"

"I don't know. He just left. He just keeps trying to find answers."

"It will be OK mom; it's just going to take time."

Meagan returned home and placed the box of Drew's things in his room, then packed the remainder of his clothes into a box that would go the boy in need. She left his Cub Scout uniform hanging in the closet beside his Boy Scout uniform. She carefully placed the small box of Drew's personal items on the shelf. Lying on Drew's bed, she looked at the ceiling.

"Where is your wallet Drew? Did someone at Gary's take it? Did you plan on taking your life? No, I don't think so. Why did you take mom's car to Sheila's that night instead of driving your own van? Why were you attracted to her when she talked so negatively and used such foul language? You couldn't have been comfortable at her house with the atmosphere so bad, so why? Why? Why?"

Meagan was sitting at the table when Jeff came home from school.

"How was your day at school Jeff?"

"It went OK mom. Everyone talked about how sorry they were over Drew's death. Sheila was there. I wouldn't even look or talk to her. I can't stand her!"

"I hope you can let all of this quiet down Jeff. I know it's hard, but the sooner the kids can go on with their lives and their studies, the better off all of you will be. I know it's difficult, but nothing can change what has taken place nor bring Drew back."

"It's so hard mom! I wish I'd said and done so many things different with Drew," Jeff sobbed, sitting at the table with his hands covering his face.

"We all do Jeff," she said as she rushed over and wrapped her arms around his shaking shoulders. "We can't go back in

81

time. All we can do is learn from our past and go on. I know Drew never would have intentionally hurt us, nor would he want us to have the feelings we have right now. We have to go on Jeff, we have to."

"I know mom, but that is easier said than done. I have so many regrets. I use to try to get Drew in trouble with my dad, and then be happy over it! I guess I was jealous over him being older and getting to do more things that I could do. I don't know why I did the things I did, I just wish now that I hadn't done them!"

"I know all of us have regrets. The thing is we can't change the past, and we can't undo what we've done. We have to learn from our mistakes and not repeat them. We should live our lives to make Drew proud of us, and not do anything that would cause him pain."

The evening passed quickly. More phone calls were answered; more sympathy cards arrived in the mail. Tasks were performed in robotic motion, and time moved on.

For thou art my rock and my fortress;
therefore for they name's sake lead me, and
guide me.
Psalm 31:3

Chapter 10
Attempting to Cope

The next day their lives returned to their familiar routines: Jeff returned to school, Alex to work and Meagan to her work. Her co-workers joked trying to make the atmosphere light and bring a smile to Meagan's face. A knock on the office door startled her. A teacher from the elementary school stood with a young girl who held a single white rose.

"Mrs. Duncan," the child said, as she handed the rose to Meagan, "this is from my class, for you. We're so sorry about your son and wanted you to know we care."

Meagan fell to her knees, wrapping her arms around the child's small shoulders. Tears instantly fell on her pretty green blouse.

"Thank you sweetheart, thank you so much."

She stood, hugged the teacher, and accepted the rose. Meagan carefully placed the flower in a vase on her desk.

Drying her tears, she reflected again on how many lives were affected by Drew's death. It was a challenge to get through each hour without tears. Her stomach continually ached as she fought back hateful feelings towards Sheila and her mother.

"I can't think about this now," She whispered, "I'll think about it later."

The weekend arrived and Meagan was grateful to have time away from her work. Alex had to work and Jeff went with his father. She jumped when the phone rang.

"Hello."

"Meagan, I need you to come up and find your dad for me."

"Mom, what do you mean find dad?"

"He went out to the barn several hours ago and hasn't come back inside. I need you to find him!"

"I'll be right there mom," Meagan said as her stomach tightened.

"Why me mom, why call me? Don't you know I can't take much more pain?"

Pulling into the driveway, her stomach tightened as she stared at the barn doors. Opening the car door, she stepped out, again faced with a body that didn't want to obey her command. She had to force each step; dreading what she might find.

Keeping her head down, she slipped into the barn. Standing perfectly still, she allowed her eyes to adjust to the dim light, and then raised them to the rafters.

"Please dear God, don't let him be hanging there," she silently begged.

"Thank you Lord," a sigh of relief escaped her lips as she viewed the empty beams. Her stomach hurt. She gently rubbed it, trying to ease the pain. She heard animal sounds coming from the milking parlor. Edging closer; fear gripped her, yet she had to know what lay ahead. Entering the darkened parlor she could make out a figure sitting on a bale of hay.

"Dad, is that you?"

Turning his face towards her, he held an object in his hands for her to see. Meagan inched forward. His shoulders were shaking hard, his face red, eyes swollen.

"Oh dad, what do you have?"

"It's Drew's toy gun and holster set I bought him when he was five," he said in a broken whisper "Do you remember Meg? Do you remember how he loved it? Now he's gone." Sobs racked his body.

"I know dad, I know." Meagan wrapped her arms around him. "Drew didn't mean it, because he would never have done anything to cause you this much pain. Mom was worried about you. I think it would be best if you didn't stay away so long. It scares mom. She's worried about you dad. She is worried you're going to do something you shouldn't. You aren't, are you, going to do something stupid I mean?"

"Meagan, I have to know why this happened, why he took my gun, why he pulled the trigger."

"Dad, we might never find the answers. But we have to go on living; we have to care for the ones left. I know you're dying inside, so am I, but we have to continue with life. We can't let this eat us alive or we won't be any good to anyone. You know Drew would never want to hurt us like this. Now please, come on, let's go into the house so mom knows you're ok."

She helped him to his feet. Anger toward Sheila and her mother festered in her stomach; anger that her parents' hearts were torn apart, anger that Jeff was going through guilt and anger.

"Suicide has to be one of the cruelest forms of death, as it left everyone with unanswered questions and guilt."

"Mom," Meagan called as they entered the house, "dad's here."

"Thank you Meagan." Her mom emerged from the bedroom, Kleenex in hand, eyes red and swollen. "Come on Tom, come and have a bite to eat."

Later, after Meagan arrived home, she suddenly burst into tears.

"Dear God," she whispered, "how much more can I take?"

After several minutes of crying she dried her tears. Regaining her composure she made out a grocery list, and drove to the store. Just as she was opening the car door she noticed a young man exiting his vehicle with a jacket on identical to Drew's. Her breath caught in her throat as she hurried towards him. When she saw blond hair below his baseball cap her heart beat faster.

A smile lit her face as she reached her hand out grasping his shoulder.

"Drew?"

"What's with you, lady?" the boy questioned as he whirled around, jerking his shoulder away.

"I'm sorry; I thought you were someone else." She gasped as she looked into brown eyes, not blue.

Meagan rushed back to the car. Once inside sobs racked her body. She held her chest, trying to ease the horrific pain.

"How stupid! How could I be so stupid to think Drew could be alive? What on earth is wrong with me?"

Returning home without groceries felt like another defeat, another battle lost. Sitting at the table, she stared out the window, seeing nothing. She thought about Drew's father. They had dated for a year and a half when she became pregnant. Back then, the only choice you were given was to quit school and get married. She didn't know the full meaning of marriage vows nor what marriage involved.

It wasn't long after the wedding that she discovered her husband rarely worked a complete week at the auto factory. He sneaked money saved for rent, leaving her to face the landlord empty-handed. Coming from a very honest family that worked faithfully and paid their bills on time, she didn't know how to deal with her husband's deceits. He disappeared for several days at a time, never telling her where he was going, nor where he had been.

One and a half years of marriage, filled with collection people banging on the door, house- hold items secretly being pawned, left without a car or phone, and days without food took a toll on Meagan. He joined a motorcycle gang, worked less and remained absent for longer periods of time. She coped month after month with each situation until the night their son, Drew, became gravely ill. Swallowing her pride, she walked to a pay phone and called her parents, and asked if they would come get them.

"Maybe I shouldn't have divorced Drew's father, then he might still be alive!" A shiver ran through her body. *"Perhaps I could have gotten a job in the auto factory and supported us. I don't know, I just don't know!"*

Be careful for nothing, but in everything by
prayer and supplication with thanksgiving
let your requests be made known unto God.
Philippians 4:6

Chapter 11
Trying to Get Over it

The next morning, while Meagan was washing dishes, Alex was outside. Suddenly a gunshot pierced the silence. The glass fell from her hand, shattering on the floor. Another shot rang out. Her stomach tightened, her breathing labored as she clutched the front of the sink and looked out the window. Another shot, and then another stabbed at her heart. Her searching eyes found Alex, rifle in hands, shooting a target in the backyard.

Rushing to the side door, she entered the garage, and clutched the knob to the outside door. *"Wait"*, her mind screamed, *"think! Alex's career and hobby involves firearms. I either cope with guns, or our relationship has to end. I don't want to be without Alex. I am going to have to find a way to cope! Why, why is it always me that has to change, that has to accept things I don't want to?"*

More shots rang out as Meagan took her hand off the doorknob, turned and returned into the house.

"Damn Sheila! The stupid girl has no idea of the hell she has created for so many.

Some day I hope she suffers as we are. Some day I hope she has a child whose heart is broken and she's helpless to change the situation. Some day I hope she gets back every ounce of agony she's created for us!"

Sitting at the table, she clutched her stomach; the pains had increased in frequency and severity. For several more minutes, she jumped at each gun shot, until they ceased. Alex came into the house with a big smile on his face.

"I've got a group the size of a quarter, Meg. The new scope is right on the money." He sat down across the table from her and then noticed her red eyes: "Are you all right? Have you been crying? Oh, Meg, you've got to put this behind you and get on with life. Crying isn't going to help. I want to see smiles on your face and hear your laughter again."

"You're right, Alex, but sometimes it's easier said than done."

Meagan jumped when the phone rang: "Hi mom."

Alex waited through the long pause.

"No, it's alright mom, we'll be right there."

"What's wrong, Meg?"

"Mom's worried about dad. He walked out behind the house hours ago and hasn't come home for lunch. And she wants me to find him again. I feel drained Alex, can you go with me?"

"Yes, of course I will. Let me put the rifle away and we'll leave."

Once there, they searched the barn without success. Then they walked the fields until Meagan was exhausted. Fighting hysteria and tears, she clutched Alex's arm; her eyes pleading for understanding.

"Meg, you go back to the house and sit with your mom. I'll cross the river and search the other side. I'm sure he's fine. Go on now, I'll be there soon."

Arriving at the house, she found her mom seated at the table, Kleenex in hand, face pale, table set for lunch.

"Alex is going to look on the other side of the river mom, but I'm sure dad's all right. Alex will bring him back."

She was silent, shaking her head no, dabbing her eyes, her chin quivering. Meagan's heart was broken for her.

"I'll get things cleaned up. I'm sure it won't be long before they come home."

About forty minutes later Meagan gave a sigh of relief as she spotted Alex and her dad crossing the back yard.

"They're back mom! Dad looks fine and they're coming in the house."

Her Mother said nothing, but turned her chair to face the door when it opened.

"Dad we were so worried! Where have you been?"

Alex looked at Meagan and shook his head indicating silence. He led her dad to the table and seated him.

"It's time to go Meg."

"But," she protested as he took her arm, leading her to the door.

Once in the car Alex turned and looked at her:

"I found him across the river, sitting in Drew's little hunting shack crying. He didn't protest when I told him we needed to go home. I think he needs time alone with your mom. Somehow he's got to accept that Drew is gone and get on with life."

"It's not that easy Alex. We have questions of why this happened and guilt for not being able to have prevented it. Dad is taking it so hard and blaming himself because Drew used his gun, and was living with him... I have to wonder if Sheila and her mother are suffering as we are, although I doubt it."

"Dwelling on it won't help Meg. You've got to get over it and get on with living."

"Get over it?" She remained silent. *"How you get over your son's death? How do you get past the blame, the guilt, the hate? That's fine Alex, I will keep silent about what I am thinking and feeling. I'll get on with life, or at least make you think I am."*

For Christ also hath once suffered for sins,
the just for the unjust, that he might bring us
to God, being put to death in the flesh, but
quickened by the Spirit.
1 Peter 3:18

Chapter 12
Detective's Report

Another week passed with Meagan going through the motions at work and at home. Deer season arrived, bringing emotions not experienced before. For the first time Meagan could remember, there would be no deer camp at her dad's. The garage, where all had gathered before, now sat empty, void of laughter, venison fries, and card games. Her father decided not to hunt; the joy of the season had vanished.

Meagan smiled as she entered the grocery store. With only a few days before Thanksgiving, she was trying to be cheerful for the holiday. She noticed a group of ladies selling bake goods as a fundraiser. Reaching out to touch a container of home baked cookies, she heard a woman's voice speaking.

"Hi Meagan. I bet you'll like the taste of those babies!"

Looking up, Meagan stared into the eyes of Sheila's mother. Her stomach instantly tied into a knot. She could feel her face redden with anger and hate. Removing her hand from the cookies, she straightened her shoulders, lifted her chin, turned and walked further into the store. With hands shaking, knees starting to buckle, and eyes filling with tears, she grabbed a cart for support. Slowly she walked each aisle, wasting time, hoping Sheila's mother would be gone by the time she checked out.

After paying for the groceries, Meagan approached the area of the bake sale. Sheila's mother stood in the same place, laughing with the other ladies.

"Damn! Why can't she just go home?"

She quickly pushed her cart out the door. Hot tears flowed as she struggled to get the key into the ignition. Half way home she looked down at the speed odometer and gasped as she read 85 miles an hour. Instantly breaking, she brought the speed back to the legal limit.

"How can she laugh and have a good time? Has she forgotten how she hurt Drew, how she threw him out of her house? How he lay dead on the ground while they continued to play music and laugh. Oh, yes, of course she can, her child is still alive! Damn her!"

"Meagan my report on your son is complete," Detective Cambs said in a phone call later that day. "Your dad has called several times requesting it. However, both of you can come in together to review it. I will give you my raw report and your dad the finished one with a lot of details left out. Will this Saturday at eleven o'clock work for you?"

"Yes, yes I am sure that will work for us. Thank you Detective."

Meagan drove to her parents house and relayed the date and time to her dad. He agreed and seemed very anxious. Saturday arrived. Her dad picked Meagan up at her home and they drove to the State Police Post. Not one word was spoken on the trip. They were led up a flight of stairs, down the hallway to a door with DETECTIVE printed in gold letters on the glass panel.

"Welcome, Tom and Meagan. Please come in and have a seat. Would either of you like a cup of coffee?"

They both shook their heads no. The detective handed each a report. She could hear her father's breathing increase as he read. She began to read hers. The description of the conversations was blunt, so many swearing words, vivid testimony from Sheila on how she sought out Drew, lied about breaking up with Gary. She told how she had seduced and used him to fill the time until Gary could return or until she could leave her home and go with him.

Gary stated that Drew was his best friend. When Sheila told him that Drew was chasing after her, trying to get them to break up, Gary felt hated for Drew. When Drew found him and Sheila together and tried to explain the truth, Gary exploded. That's when he told Drew they were no longer friends. He said Drew looked at him with puppy dog eyes, tears streaming down his face and asked Gary, "Do really mean we can't be friends any longer?"

Gary told the detective that he had no idea Sheila was lying, as there had been nothing said about them breaking up. Then all hell broke loose. Sheila was screaming Drew was a liar. Her mother came into the room screaming at Drew, all of them calling him names and telling him to get out of the house.

When he returned later, Sheila and Gary were just the other side of the vehicle that his uncle was loading. They hid there when Drew demanded to speak to both of them together. At this point, Gary still believed Sheila.

Sheila was afraid of Gary learning the truth.

The uncle (John) said he didn't know what was going on; just that he had to get all of his things loaded that night and didn't have time for any bullshit. When Drew approached John, he told him to get the hell out of there, and that he wasn't going to let him speak to them. Then Drew pulled the gun out of his waistband and aimed it at the ground, and said he wasn't leaving until he talked with them together. John knew he was serious and told Drew to give him the gun. Drew refused, so John jumped off the ramp and started towards him, and that is when Drew turned towards the car, pointed the gun to his temple, and pulled the trigger.

Sheila's mother, who had been inside the house listening and watching, called Drew's grandfather. She stated Drew had been shot and to come where he was right away. No one there believed he was dead except the uncle, and he kept moving his things into the van. Music continued as did drinking and laughing.

Soon after the shooting, his Grandfather and Alex arrived, then the Police Departments from both counties, and later the Detective. There was no evidence of foul play. Drew's death was by suicide. Case closed.

Meagan glanced at her father. Tears streamed down his face. She realized her own hands were shaking. She looked at the detective; who was looking from her to her dad.

"Do either of you have any questions about the report?"

Meagan shook her head no.

Tom looked up: "I don't understand why no one cared, and I can't believe Drew just pulled the trigger. I went to the funeral director and asked about the abrasion on Drew's chin." Tom pointed to his own chin to demonstrate where the abrasion was located.

"I thought someone had struck him, but the director said the fall caused it. That it was no different that when I was going to butcher a beef and would shoot the animal in the head. It would instantly fall forward, shoving its chin into the dirt. He said the same was true with Drew, when the bullet entered his head, he instantly dropped causing his chin to shove into the dirt and remove skin."

Meagan's eyes widened, tears filled her eyes as she stared in horror. Nothing had been said about Drew's chin before.

"*Why hadn't it been brought to her attention? More questions swirled in her mind. Did someone hit Drew*"? Anger and confusion gnawed in her stomach.

"That's true Tom. As I mentioned before, the angle of the bullet was straight, entering the right temple and exiting the left. I wish I could make this easier for you, for both of you, but I can't. Suicide is difficult for families; it leaves so many unanswered questions, questions that usually can't be answered. I don't think Drew planned on taking his life, I believe it was a quick action, taken by frustration and a broken heart."

Handing the reports back to the detective, they stood, thanked him and walked out the door. Not one word was spoken between them on the way home, just silence.

For our conversation is in heaven: from
whence also we look for the Saviour, the
Lord Jesus Christ.
Philippians 3:20

Chapter 13
The Rumor

Thanksgiving arrived, family gathered, a meal was shared, tears fell and life went on. Jeff was struggling in school. His grades dropped, he hung out at school with the wrong kids, smoking and alcohol became his habits. Nothing Meagan said or did seem to make a difference. Her hate and resentment for Sheila and her mom grew as did the pain in her stomach.

The doorbell rang just as Meagan put the last decoration on the Christmas tree. It was a friend of Meagan's.

"Hi Cindy, come in."

"I'm sorry to come over unannounced Meg, but I heard some very disturbing news I thought you should know. Sheila apparently had an abortion and is claiming it was Drew's."

Meagan fell into the kitchen chair, mouth open, eyes fixed on Cindy.

"I just thought you should know, I mean, if the baby was Drew's. Oh, I also found out Gary broke up with Sheila and has permanently moved away. Can you believe it?"

"Cindy, I'm sorry, I don't mean to be rude, but I really need to be alone now. And for your information, it couldn't have been

Drew's baby. I would appreciate it if you didn't spread this rumor to anyone else."

"Well, I thought I was helping Meg. I'm sorry if I offended you. So long Meg, keep in touch."

Meagan's mind raced back to when she found a box in Drew's room with the two used condoms inside.

"No, *it couldn't have been Drew's baby. Abortion? She killed an innocent baby? Why? And why would she tell everyone it was Drew's? Wait! Of course, if Gary left her it would only make sense to blame Drew, and then she would again be the poor victim. Pregnant with the child of a deceased lover who couldn't be there to help her, leaving her no choice but to abort the pregnancy. Damn her and her lies!"*

With both hands, she clutched her stomach as pains intensified.

"Why can't everyone stop believing Sheila's lies? Oh no, mom and dad can't find out about this! What if Jeff hears this rumor? What do I do now? Every time I think I've made progress I get kicked back further. Damn Sheila and her lies!"

The next week passed without hearing another word about Sheila or the abortion. Meagan was thankful the rumor had not reached Jeff or her parents.

Christmas approached quickly. Alex received word from the court he was awarded custody of his two girls and his home beginning on January 1st. The week before Christmas he presented Meagan with an engagement ring. They set a wedding date for January 25.

She was thrilled, confused, sad, and anxious at the same time. She knew she wanted to marry Alex; however, she didn't want to leave her home or location. Jeff would have to change schools, and she knew this might be a good move, as it would get him away from Sheila and the bad influence of his friends.

She didn't know the first thing about being a stepparent, nor how the girls (ages almost 14 and 16) would accept her and Jeff (age almost 15). She also feared moving from her parents when they still needed her help.

Cease from anger, and forsake wrath: fret
not thyself in any wise to do evil.
Psalm 37:8

Chapter 14
Jeff

Christmas came and went. January arrived and Alex moved to his house with the girls. A deep loneliness seeped into Meagan's heart. Her stomach was in constant pain; her head ached most of the time. She dwelt on how Sheila and her mom should suffer for the rest of their lives. Hate was an uncommon feeling for Meagan. She didn't know how to deal with such an ugly feeling. It was consuming her, and tainting her mind, robbing her of peace.

Meagan's mother became excited for the wedding to take place, as did Alex's Mom. Meg and her friend spent a day shopping for dresses suitable for a bride and a bridesmaid. On the clearance rack they found identical dresses, knee length, one white and the other red. She decided they would be perfect if they switched the satin belts and found matching shoes. She even found herself laughing several times throughout the day.

"Can you come up and talk with your father?" Meagan's mother asked her one day.

"What about mom? What's going on with dad?"

"He keeps looking for a suicide note. He blames himself for Drew's death. I don't know Meagan; I'm just really worried about him."

"Sure mom, I'll be right there."

Meg walked to the car and once inside stared ahead.

"Darn it! I wish he could stop trying to figure out something that has no answers!"

Arriving at her parents, she spotted her dad by the barn.

"Hey dad, what are you up to?"

He leaned against the side of the barn, hung his head, shaking it no.

"We're missing something Meg. It just doesn't make sense! He would have graduated in May and joined the Army. There's no reason why he would take his life!"

"I agree dad, no reason except for a broken heart. You are going to have to accept the point that we will never know the whole truth. We can't see into another person's heart dad. The fact is that there is nothing we can do to change what has happened. We can't bring Drew back to life."

"I know Meg, but my heart is broken. It hurts all the time. All I think about is what I could or should have done. He was living with me, he used my gun!"

"That's true dad, and it's also true that he loved you and mom tremendously and would have never purposely caused either of you this pain. You have to find a way to accept what has happened and get on with life. So many people need you. Mom needs you. Dad, I need you."

He shook his head in agreement. Meagan wrapped her arms around him and squeezed. He squeezed back. Once back into the car she felt free to allow her tears to fall.

The next day the school counselor called and asked Meagan to meet concerning Jeff. Arranging to meet during her lunch hour, Meagan drove to the school. As she got out of the car, she stood next to it for several moments, visualizing Drew walking out the double doors to meet her. Tears filled her eyes and hate gripped her heart.

Inside the school building, she kept her head down to avoid Sheila, if she happened to be in the hall at the same time. Once in the counselor's office she breathed a sigh of relief.

"Mrs. Davis," the counselor began, "Jeff is having a very difficult time in school, not only in each class, but with other students. He is hanging around with a group of boys who are in trouble most of the time and I'm afraid Jeff fits right in. I know he has had a terrible ordeal to cope with, but he just can't continue on this way."

"I know he is struggling," Meagan said, as her eyes filled with tears. "At the end of this month, I am planning on getting married and moving to a new school district. I am hopeful that placing Jeff in a new school with kids that don't know him or Drew will make a good difference."

"It could, or it could make things worse for him, taking him away from the people he knows. It will mean a lot of adjustments for Jeff. He might resent the move and new challenges, or it might be just what he needs."

"I know it is a gamble," Meagan nodded her head, "but right now I see Jeff on the wrong path and refusing to change direction. Unfortunately, his father is encouraging this behavior and telling him he doesn't have to listen to Alex, his future stepfather. I don't know what the answer is. I have to try something, and hope it will be the best thing."

"And how are you doing, Mrs. Davis?" Compassion filled the counselor's eyes. "I know this has to be extremely hard on you. Is there anything I can do for you?"

"No, you have been a tremendous help. Thank you for your time and concern, I really do appreciate it."

Meagan stood, shook the counselor's hand and walked out of the office, keeping her head down to avoid contact with anyone.

"Mrs. Davis, Mrs. Davis, wait a minute!"

Meagan turned to face three young boys. She recognized them from Drew's Boy Scout Troop.

"Mrs. Davis, we just want to say hi, and tell you that we really miss Drew. We're so sorry he's gone."

"Thank you guy's, thank you so much." Meagan held the sob until she escaped the school and reached her car. Her hands shook when unlocking the door and she dropped the keys into the snow.

"Damn Sheila!" Retrieving the keys, she unlocked the door and fell into the car. Tears streamed down her face as sobs racked her body.

After a few minutes, she started the car and drove back to work. Looking into the rear view mirror, she daubed at her eyes, trying to dry the tears and fade the redness. Once inside her office, she shut her feelings down and became all business.

That evening she asked Jeff to sit with her at the table

"Jeff, I met with the school counselor today."

"Yeah, well she doesn't like me, so I'm sure whatever she said was just her opinion."

"Let's not use her opinion then, let's just use the facts. You're failing all your grades. You've made friends with the kids that are in trouble most of the time. You've become disrespectful of everyone. I know you're hurting Jeff, so am I."

"Yeah, well, you're not hurting too badly. You're getting married aren't you?"

"Yes Jeff, Alex and I are getting married," Meagan gasped, shocked at his reaction. "We'll be moving to his place with his two daughters. You can have a fresh start in a new school, and make new friends that don't get into trouble. You will have the opportunity to raise your grades and even join a sport, or the scouts. This can make a huge difference in your life Jeff, but only if you allow it to."

"I don't want to leave my friends, or my home, to move to some other stupid school!"

Meagan's eyes filled with tears as she reached her hands across the table to Jeff's. He pulled his hands away and placed them on his hips.

"Jeff, we have to go on living. We need to do what is right, what would make Drew proud of us. He never meant to hurt us. He never would have wanted you to ruin your life."

"Well, you can make me move and change schools, but you can't make me like it!"

He glared at Meagan, then went to his room and slammed the door.

"Damn Sheila! Damn her and her lies! I hope she's suffering as we are. I hope Gary is too." Placing her head on her arms, she openly sobbed. Several minutes passed before she dried her tears and started supper.

With men this is impossible; but with
God all things are possible.
Matthew 19:26

Chapter 15
Tom's Peace

A week before the wedding Megan's mom called.

"Your dad has accepted Christ, Meagan! I think he had become so desperate that his heart was opened to God. I believe everything will be ok now. It's going to take time, but at least now he will move on. I'm so glad Meagan!"

"Oh mom, that's wonderful! I agree he will be fine now."

Meg sat at the kitchen table with pen and paper and wrote a poem for her father.

Dear Grandpa,
If you really love me-then please set me free,
  Don't dwell on what was, or what could be.
Don't you see, Grandpa, I'm up here with God & a big crowd,
  Saving room for you, with me, on this big blue cloud.

Grandpa Williams is here, and Grandpa, would you believe
 The stories are bigger than you could ever conceive!
Grandma Friend tucks Mark & me in each night,
 You couldn't ask for a more loving sight.
Grandma Williams isn't crippled with arthritis anymore,
 And spends most of her time dancing across the floor.
Uncle Wayne is up and walking, without any pain at all,
 He has the energy of a young kid and never even falls.
Grandpa Friend has got everyone beat with his tall tales of game,
 Heck, you'd think he was the biggest fisherman gone down in fame!
Danny & Dana are so healthy & strong; they play & giggle all day
 And chatter a mile a minute, I can't believe what all they can say.
Oh Grandpa, don't you see how happy I am now?
 Please, let go of your grief and quit asking "why and how,"
I'm living in the most wonderful place there ever could be,
 I wish I could bring you up here for just a minute so you could see.

Then you'd never cry again over my
being gone from you,
   You would rejoice in happiness for all
that I now can do.
You're needed on earth Grandpa, and
have work to do for God above,
   Until He calls you to Heaven where
everything is peace and love.
After I died, you became born again and
changed your life.
   You have become a better person to
others and husband to your wife.
You have found our Savior and accepted
him into your life each day
   And found a church, a Pastor,
brotherhood and learned to pray.
When the time comes Grandpa, for God
to call you home at long last,
   Well by golly, have your track shoes on,
and make the trip fast!
I'll be standing by the Pearly Gates
waiting to welcome you in.
   And on that day we will be a team
again, a team that wins.
Then you can look down & see the
sorrow in the ones you left behind
   And wish you could put the
understanding of Heaven into their
mind.
I'm happy Grandpa, and it is so
wonderful here with this big crowd,

And I'm saving space for you, with me, on this big blue cloud.
Love,
Drew

She folded it, placed it in an envelope addressed to her father and placed it in the mailbox.

So that contrariwise ye ought rather to forgive him, and comfort him, lest perhaps such a one should be swallowed up with overmuch sorrow.

II Corinthians 2:7

Chapter 16
Meagan's Forgiveness

Saturday arrived, now two weeks before the wedding. Jeff had gone to his friend's house, Alex was working, and Meagan was left to pack items not in use. The pain in her stomach never let up. It grew stronger, affecting her appetite and ability to keep food down.

In Drew's room she removed the painting from the wall, then entered the closet and took the box of personal items off the shelf. She doubled over with pain. Hate boiled within, depleting her strength and sending her and the box to the floor. A flood of emotions washed over her: hate for Sheila, her mother and Gary, frustration at not being able to help Jeff, sadness for leaving her house, excitement to marry Alex, and fear of becoming a stepparent. Her body twisted in agony as tears flowed.

An hour had passed before Meagan could gain control. The house was silent. Sitting up and stretching her arms upward, she looked at the ceiling and cried out: "God help me! In the name of Jesus Christ, I'm begging you God, take this hate from me. Please let me forgive them! Forgive my sins; forgive me for whatever I did wrong with Drew. Show me how to reach Jeff and help him through this difficult time. I can't go on this way Lord, it's eating me alive. Please, please, I beg you, help me!"

She sat for several more minutes until her sobs diminished. Suddenly calm washed over her, slowly and gently, as waves lapping the shoreline. The pain in her stomach vanished. Peace filled her heart. The hateful feelings and desire for revenge vanished.

She accepted the fact that she would never know the answers to her questions. Meagan tried to remember back to when she was a teenager. She could remember how life was all about her and even though she loved others, she did put her feelings first. She didn't consider how her words or actions would result in hurting others. These bits of wisdom came with age and experience; unfortunately, people are not born with the answers to life.

"Perhaps Sheila didn't know what her lies would do to Drew or to Gary for that matter. I guess Beth was just sticking up for her daughter and probably didn't know the truth either. Then there is Gary, who was also caught in the middle. He probably regrets the entire ordeal. I have to believe that no one knew the outcome, just as Drew couldn't have known the pain and grief his action could cause us."

Meagan stood and leaned against the wall. "Thank you Lord. Thank you for hearing me, and answering my prayers. I do forgive them, as they couldn't have known what they were doing, or the outcome it would bring. Now I am free, free to live. Thank you, Lord."

Father, forgive them; for they know
not what they do.
Luke 23:34

www.ingramcontent.com/pod-product-compliance
Lightning Source LLC
Chambersburg PA
CBHW072022060426

42449CB00033B/1604